Speed,
Day Out

Grandad got some pigeons.
He put them in a pigeon house.
Rosie helped.

Speedy was Grandad's best pigeon.
She could fly very fast, and . . .
she could land on Grandad's head.

One day, Grandad took
Rosie and Mo to town.
They went on Grandad's bike.
So did Speedy.

There were lots of pigeons in town.
Rosie and Mo looked at the pigeons.
So did Speedy.
Some of them landed on Speedy's basket.

Then they flew away.
Rosie looked at Speedy.
'Speedy wants to go too,' she said.

'She can,' said Grandad and he let Speedy go.
Speedy flew away.
'Oh no!' said Rosie.
'Oh no!' said Mo.

Grandad said,
'Speedy's a homing pigeon.
She can find her way home.'

Then Grandad said,
'Let's go to the shoe shop.
Rosie needs new shoes.'
But Rosie said,
'I don't want to go to the shoe shop.
I want to look for Speedy.'

'Speedy's on her way home,' said
Grandad. 'She's a homing pigeon.'

'Can we go home?' asked Rosie.
'But you need new shoes,' said Grandad.
'Please,' said Rosie. 'Please. Please. Please!'
'OK,' said Grandad.

On the way home,
Grandad stopped the bike.
'Oh no!' he said. 'We need a new tyre.'
'We need a garage,' said Rosie.

They looked.
They couldn't see a garage.
But they could see . . .

Speedy!

Speedy landed on Grandad's head.
'You can help us, Speedy,' said Grandad.

Grandad wrote a note.

He put the note on Speedy's leg.
Then Speedy flew away.

Rosie and Mo and Grandad waited . . .

and waited.

Then Rosie saw a van.
She saw her dad and
she saw Sam's dad.

'We got the note,' said Rosie's dad.
'Speedy took it home.'
'She's a homing pigeon,' said Rosie.

Then they all went home.
And there was Speedy!

'Can we go to town tomorrow?' asked Rosie.
'I need some new shoes.'